My Name is Sugar

written by Stacy Snyder • illustrated by Anne Johnson

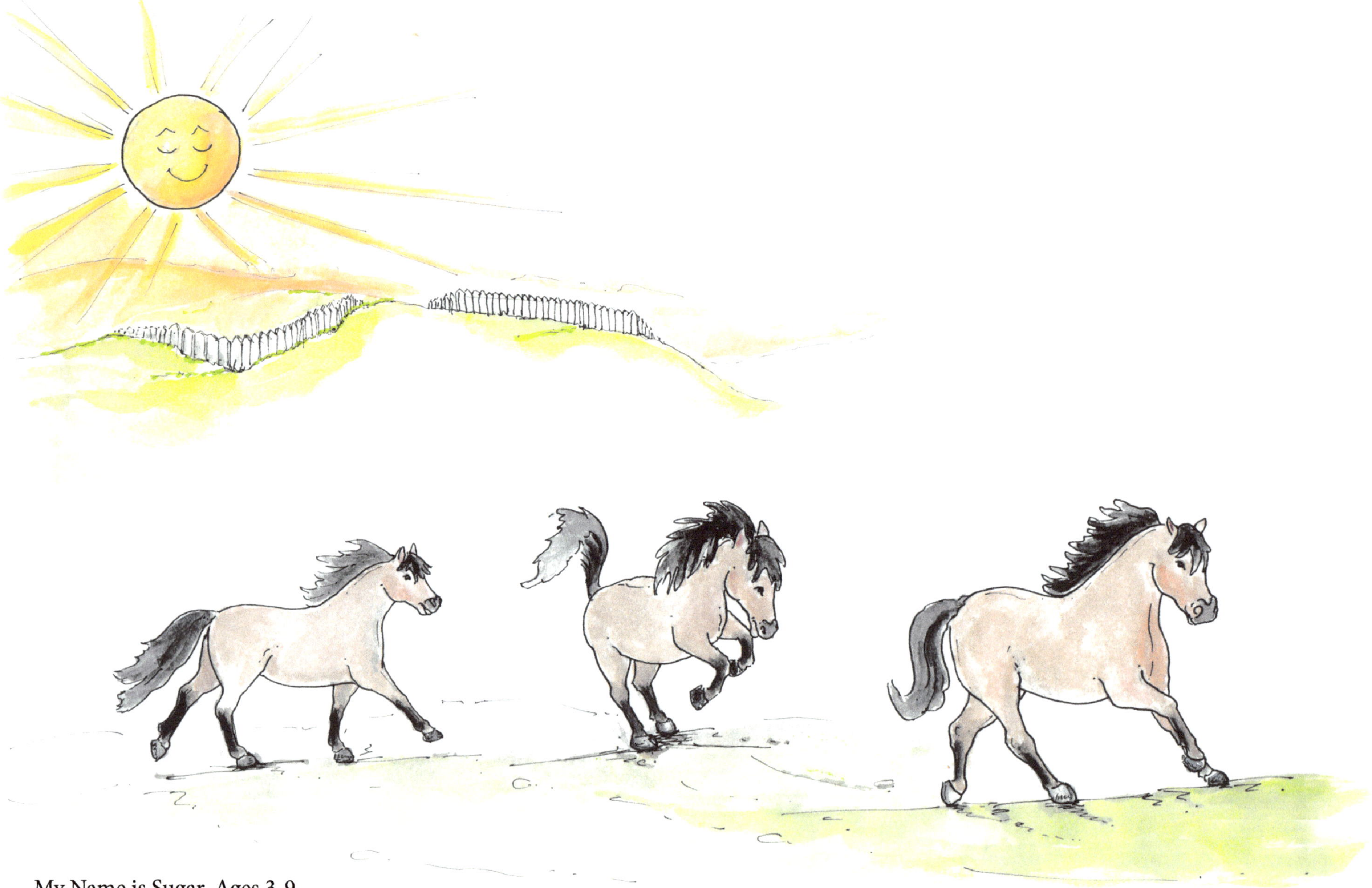

My Name is Sugar. Ages 3-9.

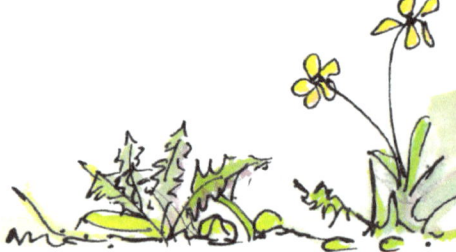

For information please contact anne@wagdesign.be or stacysnyder@mac.com
Second edition: USA 2020 ISBN: 978-0-9600041-0-2

This book is based on the true story
of two rescue animals who found each other
and became Best Friends.

1

Today, I was born. I am a miniature horse.
My parents named me Sugar.
I have a heart shaped nose. I am their sweetheart.

My mom and dad are famous show horses,
and one day they were taken away to perform.

They entertain children with
their dancing and prancing.

I started to cry as they drove away in the horse trailer.

I was left behind because I was too young and could not dance.
I was born with a crooked leg.

My mom said, "Don't worry Sugar, remember,
the light of the moon will shine upon you and
will bring us back together again."

I was left alone with a farmer who made me work very hard, pulling a cart full of heavy firewood to sell to his neighbors.

Every day I worked and worked hauling wood,
and as I got stronger so did my leg.
I was lonely in the pasture and my only friends
were the moon and the stars.

One star was brighter than all the others.
I named it Sparkle.
Sparkle watched over me at night
when there wasn't light from the Moon.
Sparkle didn't want me to be afraid of the dark.

Every night I would say,
"My special star oh so bright,
  Keep me safe throughout the night."

And with that, Sparkle would wink, "Goodnight, Sugar."

One sunny day a lady in a red hat walked by my pasture with her happy dog. The dog was so excited to see me.
Her tail was wagging back and forth, and she ran right up to me.

The lady called out, "Come, Charger!"

I was afraid.

The lady replied, "Don't be afraid, we only want to be your friend!"

But just as quickly as they had arrived, the Lady in the Red Hat and the happy dog were gone.

That night Sugar looked up to the Moon and Sparkle and asked, "Can you help me find my friends?"

Wonderful Moon, show me what to do,
with all my heart I trust in you...

Sparkle Sparkle, come and play,
shine your light to show the way.

The next day the gate to Sugar's pasture was left open.

This was her chance to escape and find the Lady in the Red Hat
and the dog she called Charger!

She ran into the forest, not knowing which way to go.
She ran and ran and ran and soon became very tired and hungry.
Sugar found a quiet clearing among the trees to lie down,
eat some grass, and get some much needed rest.

12

Suddenly, Sugar was awakened
by the most unusual sound.

RIBBIT

RIBBIT

There it was,
a TREE FROG.

"Who are you?" asked Sugar.

13

"My name is Sticker!"
croaked the frog.

"Nice to meet you Sticker.
My name is Sugar,
and I am looking for my new friends.

Can you help me?" asked Sugar.

Sticker replied,
"That's wonderful, I would love to help you!"

"All you need to do is wait until the sun sets,
and the crescent Moon rises in the night sky.
Then, underneath the Moon you will find what you are looking for!"

Sugar stayed in the forest with Sticker and every night
they watched and waited for the Moon to rise in the night sky.
Each night the Moon would change in size.
Days later, after Sugar and Sticker had waited patiently,
the crescent Moon appeared, it was so beautiful. The sky was lit up
by a sea of brilliant stars with Sparkle in the middle.

Sugar knew it was time for her to leave Sticker,
so she headed out into the night in search of her new friends and new home.

By the time the Moon had set,
and the sun had risen,

Sugar found herself standing
in a beautiful garden.

18

Sugar looked up; she couldn't believe her eyes.
There was the Lady in the Red Hat and the dog she called Charger.

The lady reached out to Sugar and said,
"Don't be afraid, we have been waiting for you
and we want you to be our friend."
The two jumped up and down with joy.

Charger had found
the friend she had been hoping for...

...and Sugar had found the friend
she had always been looking for.

That night,
Sugar and Charger looked up at the sky;
the Moon was full and bright.

Charger barked,
Sugar whinnied,
Sparkle winked,
and the Moon smiled.

They were all so happy to finally be together.

Follow the adventures of Sugar and Charger in their next book,

The Sugar Shack.

Now go back and see if you can spot any of these friendly little creatures.

STACY SNYDER is a graduate of the University of Arizona, with a degree in Special Education. She resides in San Diego, California, with her loving husband John. She is the mother of two daughters, and the grandmother of four beautiful grandchildren. Her background in education and love for nature were the inspiration for this book. She was taken by the extraordinary relationship that developed between a rescued dog and a rescued miniature horse. Their unconditional love is a heart-warming example of kindness.

ANNE JOHNSON has been painting and illustrating her entire life and received her Master's degree in Medical Illustration from the Medical College of Georgia. She has a great love of animals and nature and has been passionate about children's books since she was a young girl. Born and raised in Minnesota, she currently resides in Belgium and is the proud mother of three loving teenagers, a dog, a rabbit, two cats, and two horses. *My Name is Sugar* is her first children's book.

SUGAR is a rescued buckskin miniature horse. She was in very poor shape when she was adopted. Scared and very skittish. With patience and spending lots of time with her, she has become a loving, contented horse with the help of her friend Charger. Age unknown.

CHARGER was adopted as a puppy, and has grown into a large, strong dog with a very happy disposition. Charger loves to go on walks with her best friend Sugar on a double leash. She also insists on wearing sunglasses. Charger is 9 years old.

*This book is dedicated to
the beautiful children, grand-children, cousins, nieces and nephews
that have all played an important part in its development.*

*Without the loving support from this close-knit family
and the special bond between the author and the artist,
this book would not have been possible.*

Printed in the USA
CPSIA information can be obtained
at www.ICGtesting.com
LVHW071940090823

754487LV00001B/2